P9-COO-998

FOOTBALL'S
GREATEST
STARS

J. J.
WATT

by Matt Scheff

SportsZone
An Imprint of Abdo Publishing
abdopublishing.com

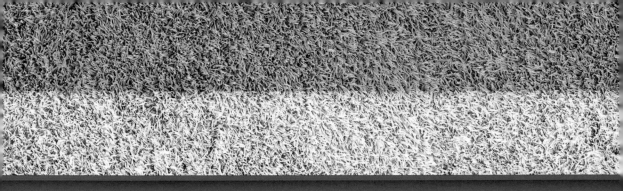

abdopublishing.com

Published by Abdo Publishing, a division of ABDO, PO Box 398166, Minneapolis, Minnesota 55439. Copyright © 2016 by Abdo Consulting Group, Inc. International copyrights reserved in all countries. No part of this book may be reproduced in any form without written permission from the publisher. SportsZone™ is a trademark and logo of Abdo Publishing.

Printed in the United States of America, North Mankato, Minnesota
042015
092015

THIS BOOK CONTAINS
RECYCLED MATERIALS

Cover Photos: Aaron M. Sprecher/AP Images (foreground);
Scott A. Miller/AP Images (background)
Interior Photos: Aaron M. Sprecher/AP Images, 1 (foreground), 24-25, 26-27; Scott A. Miller/AP Images, 1 (background); Greg Trott/AP Images, 4-5, 6-7; Scott Boehm/AP Images, 8-9, 18; Robin Alam/Icon SMI, 10-11; David Stluka/AP Images, 12-13; Carlos Osorio/AP Images, 14-15; Andy Manis/AP Images, 16-17; Morry Gash/AP Images, 19; Zuma Press/Icon SMI, 20-21; Tony Gutierrez/AP Images, 22-23; David J. Phillip/AP Images, 28-29

Editor: Nick Rebman
Series Designer: Jake Nordby

Library of Congress Control Number: 2015932402

Cataloging-in-Publication Data
Scheff, Matt.
  J. J. Watt / Matt Scheff.
    p. cm. -- (Football's greatest stars)
Includes index.
ISBN 978-1-62403-828-0
1. Watt, J. J., 1989- --Juvenile literature. 2. Football players--United States--Biography--Juvenile literature. 3. Defense (Football)--Juvenile literature. I. Title.
796.332092--dc23
[B]   2015932402

CONTENTS

DIVISION CHAMPIONS

Late in the 2012 season, the Houston Texans needed a win to clinch their division. Defensive end J. J. Watt made sure they would not miss the chance.

The Indianapolis Colts had the ball at Houston's 1-yard line. Colts running back Mewelde Moore took the handoff and crashed into the line. Watt punched the ball out of Moore's hands, causing a fumble. Houston recovered!

FAST FACT
Watt started a charity that helps to provide after-school athletic activities for children.

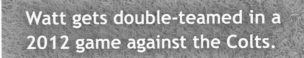

Watt gets double-teamed in a 2012 game against the Colts.

Watt did not stop there. He stuffed running backs for lost yardage. He swatted down passes. And he sacked quarterback Andrew Luck three times.

Watt's play made it all but impossible for the Colts' offense to move the ball. At the end of the game, Watt and his teammates celebrated a 29-17 victory, an AFC South division title, and a ticket to the playoffs.

Watt dives toward Colts quarterback Andrew Luck.

FAST FACT

Watt had a league-leading 20.5 sacks during the 2012 season.

EARLY LIFE

J. J. Watt was born on March 22, 1989, in Waukesha, Wisconsin. Hockey was his first love. He started playing at age four. But J. J. gave up hockey at age 13. It was getting too expensive.

J. J. turned to other sports. In high school, he starred in track and field, basketball, and baseball. But football was his real passion.

FAST FACT

Watt's initials, J. J., stand for Justin James.

Watt chases the ball carrier in a 2009 game against Northwestern.

J. J. was a star on both sides of the ball. He played tight end on offense. On defense, he was a defensive end. He was named the Most Valuable Player (MVP) of his high school team.

But J. J. was not a highly rated college prospect. He did not get offers from any colleges that were football powers. He finally accepted a scholarship from Central Michigan.

FAST FACT

In 2007 J. J. won the Wisconsin high school state championship in the shot put.

Watt runs down Ohio State quarterback Terrelle Pryor.

BIG DECISIONS

At Central Michigan, Watt mainly played tight end. In 2007 he caught only eight passes all season. The coaches suggested that he switch to the offensive line.

Watt did not want to make that switch. The next year, he left Central Michigan and enrolled in a community college. He took a job delivering pizzas.

Watt lunges toward a running back during a 2010 victory over Minnesota.

FAST FACT

Central Michigan finished the 2007 season as champions of the Mid-American Conference.

One day while Watt was delivering pizzas, a young boy recognized him. The boy asked Watt why he was not playing football. The question stuck with Watt.

He transferred to the University of Wisconsin and tried out for the football team. The coaches let him join the Badgers as a walk-on.

Watt runs with the ball after intercepting a pass at Michigan.

FAST FACT

Watt has two younger brothers, both of whom went on to play football for the Badgers.

Watt delivers a hard tackle to Purdue running back Ralph Bolden in 2009.

Watt gave up on becoming a tight end. Instead he focused on being a defensive end. In 2008 Watt helped lead Wisconsin's scout team. But he never got to play in an actual game.

He finally got that chance the next year. Watt made the most of it. In 2009 he recorded 44 tackles and 4.5 sacks.

FAST FACT
Watt also did well in the classroom, earning Academic All-Big Ten honors.

In 2010 Watt broke out as one of the best defenders in college football. His rare combination of strength, size, and speed made him a terror on defense. He could rush the quarterback, stuff running backs, and drop back in coverage.

Watt and the Badgers went 11-1 in the regular season. They were the Big Ten co-champions.

Watt pursues the ball carrier in a 2009 game at Camp Randall Stadium.

Watt holds a rose in his mouth after helping the Badgers earn a trip to the Rose Bowl.

FAST FACT

Watt was named Wisconsin's team MVP in 2010.

GOING PRO

Many teams in the National Football League (NFL) were impressed with Watt's overall game. So he left college a year early to enter the 2011 NFL Draft. The Houston Texans selected him with the eleventh overall pick.

Many rookies struggle to keep up with the size and speed of NFL players. But Watt was different. During his first season, he had 5.5 sacks and helped Houston reach the playoffs for the first time.

FAST FACT
As a rookie, Watt started all 16 of Houston's games.

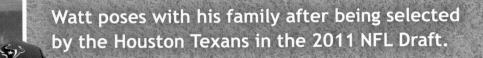

Watt poses with his family after being selected by the Houston Texans in the 2011 NFL Draft.

Watt was better than ever
in the playoffs. The Texans
faced the Cincinnati Bengals
in the first round. The game was
tied 10-10 with less than a minute
to go in the second quarter. Bengals
quarterback Andy Dalton dropped
back and threw a pass.

Watt snatched the football out
of the air. Interception! Watt then
sprinted 29 yards to the end zone.
His touchdown gave Houston the
lead for good.

Watt celebrates after returning an
interception for a touchdown during
a playoff game against the Bengals.

FAST FACT
Watt was named to *Pro Football Weekly's* All-Rookie Team in 2011.

Watt's career was off to a great start. Yet no one could have guessed what was in store for him in 2012. At times, it seemed like no one could block him. He blasted through offensive lines for 20.5 sacks. And when he was not making tackles, he was swatting down passes. His ability to knock down passes has earned him the nickname "J. J. Swatt."

Watt tries to pump up the crowd during a 2012 game.

FAST FACT

Watt was named the 2012 NFL Defensive Player of the Year. Some experts called his season the best ever by a defensive player.

BUILDING A LEGACY

After a solid 2013 season, the Texans rewarded Watt with a six-year, $100-million contract. That made him the highest-paid defender in NFL history.

In 2014 Watt proved that he was worth it. He matched his career high with 20.5 sacks. He also earned his second NFL Defensive Player of the Year Award.

FAST FACT

Watt got a chance to play tight end for the Texans in 2014. He caught three passes, and all of them were touchdowns!

Watt battles with a Denver Broncos lineman during a game in 2013.

In a span of four years, Watt went from delivering pizzas to becoming one of the NFL's biggest stars. The league has rarely seen a player with his set of skills.

When Watt steps onto the field, all eyes are on him. Whether he is sacking quarterbacks, batting down passes, or catching touchdowns, J. J. Watt is always capable of making big plays.

Watt raises his arms to celebrate a sack against the Baltimore Ravens.

FAST FACT

In 2014 Watt was named to the Pro Bowl for the third straight year.

TIMELINE

1989
J. J. Watt is born on March 22 in Waukesha, Wisconsin.

2007
Watt graduates from high school and attends college at Central Michigan.

2008
After one season, Watt leaves Central Michigan. He joins the Wisconsin Badgers as a walk-on.

2009
Watt starts all 13 games for the Badgers.

2010
Watt leads the Badgers to a Big Ten co-championship and is named the team's MVP.

2011
The Houston Texans select Watt with the eleventh pick in the NFL Draft.

2012
Watt records 20.5 sacks and 16 passes defended, and he earns the NFL Defensive Player of the Year Award.

2014
Watt signs a $100-million contract extension before the season and wins his second Defensive Player of the Year Award.

GLOSSARY

COVERAGE
The act of defending receivers and trying to prevent them from catching passes.

PROSPECT
An athlete likely to succeed at the next level.

ROOKIE
A first-year player.

SCHOLARSHIP
Money given to a student to pay for education expenses.

SCOUT TEAM
A unit that helps the starters prepare for upcoming opponents.

TRANSFER
To move to a new school.

WALK-ON
A player on a college team who does not receive a scholarship for participating.

INDEX

ABOUT THE AUTHOR

Matt Scheff is an artist and author living in Alaska. He enjoys mountain climbing, deep-sea fishing, and curling up with his two Siberian huskies to watch football.